NIGHT AND DAY

Night and Day

Pierre Alferi

translation by
Kate Lermitte Campbell

LA PRESSE 2012 :: IOWA CITY & PARIS

Sentimentale Journée by Pierre Alferi
Copyright © 1997 P.O.L Éditeur
Translation copyright © 2012 by Kate Lermitte Campbell
All rights reserved

Published in the United States by La Presse,
an imprint of Fence Books

La Presse/Fence Books are distributed by Consortium
www.cbsd.com
www.lapressepoetry.com

Library of Congress Cataloguing in Publication Data
Alferi, Pierre, 1963 —
Translated from the French by Kate Lermitte Campbell
Night and Day/Pierre Alferi
p.   cm.

ISBN 978-1-934200-58-2
1. French poetry. 2. Poetry. 3. Contemporary translation.

Library of Congress Control Number: 2012931616

First Edition
10 9 8 7 6 5 4 3 2 1

We would like to give warm thanks to
Paul Otchakovsky-Laurens and P.O.L, who first published
this work in book form, for letting us publish this translation.
www.pol-editeur.com

NIGHT AND DAY

Contents

The day advances masked
The strongest subtlest feeling
Of the day
The night
Lays its mechanisms bare
The burden of time
Water's coming in, we're heading straight
For the iceberg.

So the day advances masked
On very narrow rails. Oh no,
It doesn't look its age, which doesn't mean
It's older. Were it enough to hold
A mirror to the overbearing light
To read back to front across it — what? Not the truth
All the same. Just that the kilo of tomatoes
Weighs a bit more or less. The hum
Of the town directs the boom from one minute to the next
Following the days chorus, frail-sounding
Through riffs of oiled brass. The rendition
Smells of sweat and the big band in ragged tails
Mocks a classical orchestra. — No, no, that coat of mail
Couldn't suit you better, I swear. — I'm not saying
It clashes, but what if we dance? The man next to you
Doesn't find the music modern enough, he's a magazine
Reader. — So in three years you'll no longer love
The things you love today. — No
It's not that simple. I like, says your neighbor, things that give me

The strongest subtlest feeling
Like a perfume crossing the room on stiletto
Heels, of the day. Later
When I pop the cork I know
(And this adds spice to my pleasure
A bit bland as yet) that it'll be there
Vintage. — I see. That sort of thing never happens
To me I'm afraid, or only thanks to desperately
Vaporous creatures. Water that boils just
Before rising in the coffee pot, the sun
When it spills over the stained carpet
The fork clinking against the pewter
Of a plate of scraps for the cat drives him nuts.
For example. And that, you see, doesn't have much to do
With culture. I no longer read. Well
No longer hoping to feel — what? To feel
Quite simply. Some people put their polaroids
In the freezer; they age badly, that's obvious, but
Don't mistake the desire to postpone effacement
For that of unreal colours. Iceberg, aurora borealis.
Time only flows colorless at room
Temperature. As soon as the atmosphere coagulates
It stinks of cooking oil. The dishwasher has made
Thin scales as strange as fragments of meteorite
With more human remains. There are days
Like that. That'll be enough for this one
OK? Anyway the light is falling suddenly
In the bar, signalling a change of tariff

And daylight saving time, what a con, launders
Evening's loot by taxing morning sleep.
— Good night, sleep well my love. — If that's an order
Rest assured I'll mutiny. The captain's at the back of the hold.
A cat couldn't find her kittens in this murk
And neither the port we left nor the one we're heading for
Is visible. Yesterday stood me up. Tomorrow
Tomorrow (*Gone with the wind*)
Is another day. Night-time, what unexpected
Violence, don't you think? You're sleeping.
Not that it evokes death, the haunted solitude
Of children — these thoughts will populate insomnia —
But it lays yesterday's mechanisms bare
On the deck the whole ocean transforms itself
Into a machine room and at each lookout post
The amorphous discontinuity of hours tortures
The ship's boy. If only he'd known! Not an interesting
Angst, Heidegger-style, as
That sleep-deprived friend says: a shambles, a sadistic medley
Of the worst songs on Golden Oldies AM,
The burden of time. Do you see that someone
Longs to wake you, my love, to grasp
Your shoulders to show you the dreadful things going on?
— What is it? — There's water coming in, we're heading straight
For the iceberg, and no, there's nothing on the horizon, that's just
The horror of it. Some say the *Titanic*
Never sank, but another
Almost identical ship; that its corrupt owner

13

Sold its name, counting on a shipwreck with no dead
To cash in on the insurance. The *Titanic* — the real one —
Would still be anchored in some peaceful harbor
No one knows where. A postcard exists
Showing a half-sunk steamship — the *Cabiria*
Or perhaps the *Carribbean* — with this caption in bold:
'You are invited.' It had something to do with the inauguration
Of a restaurant. I wondered who to send it to for ages,
Definitely a woman. I admit that I feel quite an affinity
With this renamed boat stripped of its big band
That sank, sinks still in our minds and
Never sank. Most often in the evening: evenings
Are so sentimental. I still have that card.
You've earned it through the toil of your sleep.

Put
A date to this face
A price on this memory
They're floating in the indirect
Light of communication
They are euphemisms
A dream
We only saw
The smoke, too late to put a word
To the Thing
Hostage of litotes.

Put a voice to her prose
Said the ad. You'd have called it
A spoonerism. The tarty blond image
Goes neither with the second noun
Nor with the first. But the invite's cunning
Even when you know that this body, these mass-typed
Promises, this organ ready to make you pay
With loving words early as six A.M.
On your credit card belong to at least
Three different people. The game
Is in the countess's album to fit a head
On a chest, legs into typografolkloresque costumes
And all the cards turn over. Put
A date to this face, to see, a code
On this account, a price on this memory.
And if you give the same answer — the same
As what? — the same statistically you'll have

Won — what? — the bag of answers in the epistolary
Chain. The caricature also hits on the mean
Deadens interference, effaces failed shots
All free. Just now at the end of the line
She's asking why the supervisory staff
Never ever marry aurally challenged
Physically disabled colored cleaners.
This morning the passers-by have chins stuck
With shaving cream, eyes half open, their steps
Slightly slowed. They're floating in the indirect
Light of communication. Perhaps
Because you slept badly their words were
Translated several times by machines
Before ending up in this cul-de-sac. They too
Are euphemisms and won't help at all
In gathering up the night's scraps of hemp, the bits
Of dry tobacco already in the Rizla + roller:
At the beginning you always take too much, the morsels
Tender at first block it up
Heard voices closed eyes metallize
Run on empty. Don't imitate speech
When writing, don't put your drenched boots back on
They said. Not really a metaphor: a dream
And this other one: History rising drowned everything
Leaving only a few names and bells above water, plus some divers
Writing a thesis on dustbins. — But what is
That baby doing on the roof? How did it get there?
You who are interested in voices you say

It's a question of finding a name for it. I leave
That job to Noah when he passes
With the dustmen. Duty calls: to retrace
The cloudy submarine story that explains nothing
But makes the link. It happened between two shadows
Beneath the dark line of contrast. The dancer
On the blue pack of tobacco should have guessed
That you don't hunt for a screwed up bill expecting to get away with it
In the flickering light thrown by that sort of film.
Steps resound, stop, resound
And the crime takes place off-screen. We only saw
The smoke. Too late to put a word
To the Thing responsible and the victim carries
Her stage name with her into sleep. Mine
Was therefore produced by Val Lewton. Is she
Still on the line, the hostage of litotes?
The reply she gets is sorry but the call cannot
Be put through yet please hold the
Line. She prefers to call back later.

It's wonderful
Not to know where things come from
Hidden sequences
Are finer
There are intrigues in the midst of which you forget
The beginning, no longer anticipate the end
For another moment or so
Everything is penetrable.

It begins like that, in the middle
Of a conversation: the market has already blossomed
In the burning hot square
The budding phase
And to call this town
Venice it was necessary to camouflage
The infrastructure, to place
Forks knowingly
Spillikins over the orchestra pit.
The merchandise brought in
By convoys without headlights
Silently at night
Rivals nature.
Give us our money back! Yet it's wonderful
Not to know where things come from
Not even children and when ethnologists
Pose as missionaries
Of family planning
To laugh with the savages.

Hidden sequences
Are finer. If you grasp them, lift them
By the neck like poisonous
Snakes, sticks
Entwined, many sentences
Are compatible. Their jaws
Open so wide beneath the pressure of your fingers
If necessary, another tube
Slots in and all the plumbing
Gets going with liquid joints.
What is it that gives this morning
With its well-punctuated accidents
Of the market, the café, the return to the dark-room
The cohesion of a film? Not the music
Stuck on top, redundant, the shame
Of cinema. No, a prosody, improvised
Perhaps, which doubles back
On itself nonchalantly. Impossible to tear it away
From its pretext, it will pollute
The air, the film alone remaining
On walls and skin. Molded brass:
A link between two movements
Hidden between two currents. That's how
It begins, when the journey's underway. That's pretty much
What I mean. — But it makes no sense
My poor friend. — Fine. There are intrigues
In the midst of which you forget
The beginning, no longer anticipate the end: gangsters on the run

Place themselves like paper sumo wrestlers
On a cardboard platform but it's just a circle
Traced in the sand on the beach. So
Their associates beat the ground with the flats of their hands:
They fall still rigid, the reel turns faster
The spectators tremble in their seats
Until one of them crosses
The line. Fine art. What could you do
Today that would be better than to raise
The miniature to the real size of the game?
Miniscule fragments stretch themselves out
The breakdown vehicle here to save us is held together with rubber bands.
That happened for no reason at all
On our journey
Towards death. The tardy explorer
In mid descent of the Orinico or the Amazon
Develops a fever, paralysed he watches the sliding
Of an interminable snake, the mouth seems
As distant as the source. Or
Sitting in the middle of a tree trunk, look
He remarks that it's a crocodile.
Such things happen in life: halfway through
In the ambiguous zone where for another moment or so
Everything remains amorphous, penetrable —
or so you would like to believe.
Anonymous well-wishers make sure ends meet
Fill the stalls' empty boxes but we must
Hope that when night comes the dildos will adapt

To the universal harness. That's how
It begins, that's how
I understand it provided that no conductor
Decides to tap the rostrum with his stick
And that no date is fixed.

MAN'S FAVORITE SPORT

No proof
That we're advancing
Doubt
Insinuated itself
That's when
I admitted that a good thing might not be good
You say
That happiness is one thing and sadness
Another the two compatible
Let's move on.

So? Happy? I was joking
We're now driving on the flat
Between two luminous crates of jungle
We've caught the scent of home. Even before
We'd turned round, sounded each other out
A crowd of delirious students clamored for
Our first impressions. — This voyage
Has no scientific value. No proof
That we're advancing. Something definitely came out
Of the foam thanks to the excessive hygrometry
Of the region and its waters
So profuse that they spit fish lacking lures
Alas we're pathetic mycologists
And our art of fishing is purely academic.
We discover interesting samples
Of lava in dusty shop windows
We obtain them at low prices but
Don't think of melting them down

To extract the pendulum, the abbreviated message.
Ah we make a good couple when one
Catches up with the other. Doubt
Insinuated itself — do you remember? —
When we ended up in that forest of parasol mushrooms.
Your hair was in a bit of a mess, I still had
My cap with earflaps, my jacket
And my tweed knickerbockers with leather braces.
— First-rate, I said and there were you on tiptoe
To reach the ring the bitter aftertaste warned you
That it's poisonous. The catch, what's more,
Didn't really conform to the rules. — I remember
The minimal credit accorded by the budding scholar
I was to my mother when she said I had
Eyes bigger than my stomach. We were
Punished for our delusions of grandeur
That led us to sin but in an infinitely small way
Catching a purulent mycosis. That's when
I admitted that a good thing might not be good
And I never went back on it.
To say that for that it was necessary
Free and bound tightly, given over
One to the other to descend
To the center of the Earth
Where the museums are shut, buses no longer circulate
To be tossed out to the antipodes
On a shell bed. Anyway
The landscape's unchanged, the grocer makes it his duty

To speak to us as though he saw us yesterday.
— Just a light fluttering
Between sky and subsoil, I wouldn't call
That dry land. Of course
I knew you had a soul
And fluctuations within it. You say
That happiness is one thing and sadness
Another, the two compatible. That's beyond my domain.
The shadows of those iguanas follow us
Disguised and fattened like amanita (parasol mushrooms!)
Through a game of perspective: no danger.
The word 'real' in your mouth closes
The back door. Calm, I will be completely
When we've put a few cable lengths
Between them and him. Let's move on
To your English revision lesson.
You say: *it was a nice journey*
I translate: une bonne journée.

AS THOUGH NOTHING WAS GOING ON

Four themes then
Déjà-vu
Sexual ambiguity
Verse & prose
My birthday
And blurred contours are unavoidable.

You'll hold to
Spring or autumn
Her and him
Mac of prose and pleated
Skirt of poetry
This cinematic triplet
You say the loved one alone
Forms a pair

A place already
Known without being
Known because of the twist
In the path of the
Cut yes the same
Day of the year
You don't know where to stand
In the room
Reflected you see

Nothing to say to
This day apart
Apart from that when taking a step
Back, steps
Not necessary
An intrigue takes shape
Has taken shape though
We never wove it
Less than a private
Story ball of wool
Squashed
On square
One

Strange concetto
You've been warned there are
Four themes then
Déjà-vu
Sexual ambiguity
Verse & prose
And blurred contours are unavoidable

Why call it
Love carp
The waiter says mute
How will she express
Her feelings
And my friend

There's no rule
Concerning our preferences

Middle-aged
Do you hope that Glen or Glenda
Will remain suspended
With no patronymic nor
Job de-
Generated
As for this body
Clothed in chives and garlic
Fish or fowl
We'll make do
With that explanation

There's no question of hesitation
The cards are well placed
This life you
Pleated skirt this rhythm
Nothing else but

Tough luck for those who don't appreciate
The way you cross lines at the slightest
Opportunity, consume
With moderation
And the priggish pedantry of a vague oenologist
The choice comprises
Like this angle

Looking onto the room
All others
Or not? Was it
Just a desire a refusal
Of time you find
Too much equivocation
You can't even
Count on the
Weather these days

At home finally
Something is
Different the same
The armchair or
The table oh I've got it
You've put the table
And the armchair
Where they were a few
…Months ago?
A few months ago.

THE DEMON OF SUBTLETY

It's not this time not yet
That I'll manage to tell you what you thought I might
It's time for your next date
He blows
Everything out of proportion and then
Nitpicks
I don't like that man.

Fine, I'll let you go. It's not this time not yet
That I'll manage to tell you what you thought I might
One way or another. Luckily the wait
Has many strings to its bow in this garden which between
Flocks of crows, families of starlings, the blackbirds
And Japanese cherry trees that bleach their shadow
Doesn't lack international attraction. Anyhow
It's time for your next date, I can see him coming.
I'd recognize him from two hundred meters away
Just because he never seems to be getting closer
Tracing zigzags between the flowerbeds, turning
His head in every direction except the right one
Like that tit on the ground on its guard
Because on the ground a plane isn't quite a plane
Nor a tit a tit. The meanders of the alpine enclosure
Below have added folds to the brain
And differences in height the Himalayan miniature
Towering over the Chinese one, the pond that is Baikal Lake
With one meter fifty of steppe and Gullivian travellers
Who pass each other unwittingly separated by dwarf trees

On three terraces. He pretends not to have seen you
Afraid of being early and when he shakes your hand
It will crown a strange bow
Turret-like, one foot back, one arm behind
Chin raised in profile. If I can
Give you some advice, don't whatever you do tell him
A story he'll tell back to you.
He loves puzzles and search inventories so much
That I reckon he's quite happy contemplating lists
Twitching with pleasure and never collating them.
At school he was called the angel of weird
Or — because when asked 'how's it going?' he replied
Either, paralyzed with scruples, 'I'm dead,' or
As he began all responses, 'It's complicated' —
Mr. Valdemar. The population
Flutters a bit too much now, the phrases
Of birds fuse each suspended
In its own ether. I hear them conversing
Like finer and finer comparisons never-ending
But of different types. There isn't, there never
Will be an interpreter polyglot enough
And the man looks like a volatile hybrid to which
All others are deaf, a chimera sterile
As a mule. Watch him zigzag
Between dahlias and thoughts like a pinball
Like a fish out of water, like, like.
I doubt he's ever caught anything when hunting amongst
The labelled plants, the giant crystals: he blows

Everything out of proportion and then
Nitpicks. Strange creature the blackbird, at once
So brutal and so persnickety. I'm going I'm going. While waiting
He lost you in all the detail. Between you the path
Isn't long but it twists. As you make up
For lost time it becomes easier to see the richness of the flowerbeds
That the date pushes up within you, the wait grows,
Branches out, buds, you rehearse the luxurious
Conversations to follow, though time turns too
The quadrangle of ryegrass becomes once again a Jurassic forest
Through which you advance machete in hand. We'll be wiser on the other side
Stronger and more intelligent, inspired, entwined yes
Like liana but you never get anywhere
With techniques like that or so late or so
Exhausted that you can't say anything about it. — Where were you?
Where had he gone? — Just nearby and that's the worst excuse.
Since two and two make four you'd think he wasn't
In a rush to see you again. If it occurs to him to tell you he loves you
Don't panic he'll begin with the weather
Like the man without qualities then he'll depart
Suddenly feeling he's been quite direct
Leaving you deep in an exasperated sleep.
The natural cacophony, the gaudy bouquets explode
Burst your eardrums, hurt your eyes, grate on your nerves.
Such a pretty garden ruined by a mania.
I'm exaggerating? At least I'll have tried to distract you
Talking simply as you waited (for him)
Taking no detours but one. You're now going to re-ascend

31

The alley to the entrance despite the reverberation
And the thread of Byzantine warblings to the strangely shaped
Fruit that emits them at regular intervals.
I don't like that man. I am that man.

FOLLOWING OUR CONVERSATION

Call that
The trace of memory, the trace of private speech
What is it that hasn't
Happened
What is it that matters, exists
Really? These spoken, written, sung things
Or their formless echo
You can recreate
Music with
What attention
Or rather what distraction?

Following our conversation
The other day a buzzing started
Like a wasps' nest inhabited by a single wasp
Old and very cautious. Discovered she would be
Done for, she knows it. With no guarantor her bustling activity
Is no longer justified and stops as soon as
Someone's listening, she can feel it. Sometimes the bzz
Of the fridge provides a cover or perhaps the pff
Of pipes in the wall or the neighbor's vacuum cleaner.
The voice migrates towards them, a pianist hums
Mechanically the monophonic mental mushy version
Of what his fingers are playing — imagine two hands blurred as one
A thumb on each side, a reverse shot
Doubled. What a mess! Yet at least one thread, just one
Sound keeps on behind the clear dialogue, its perfect execution
Like a shameful pirate shadow. Call that
The trace of memory, the trace of private speech —

After days and nights in the studio balancing the sound
Going slowly mad you put the tape
In the car-park bloody freezing on an ancient car radio
— What's happened? What is it that hasn't
Happened? Doubtless one part of the pre-recorded debate
Was cut down more than the other broadcast out to
One of the debaters lounging in his socks
His tie undone by his set. And even
If deep inside he thinks the other man's right
You can bet your bottom dollar that the most contorted arguments
Aren't his. In the street this morning
The well-dressed man waving his handkerchief before his mouth
To hide the furious statements directed within
Seems to me to let just one predominate.
— What counts most? What is it that matters, exists
Really? These spoken, written sung things
Or their formless echo when you turn your head
The subliminal choir sitting at the back?
The echo is feeble, its peak low, but it isn't
Simple (= 1 fold), you can unfold it in the labs
Receivers of the creased damp faded bills that have been
Through the wash in trouser pockets. You can make
Music with it, write on the back of a shopping list
Not just silly bits of conversation
But their sillier prolongations. — What attention
Or rather what distraction is necessary to hear nothing
But a background noise and not aggravate
The secret studio behind the trompe-l'oeil wall

The little hands and archaic machines
Whisked away at the drop of a hat on the slightest suspicion of descent
Or slightly lengthened stare? It's not the hunter
But his apathetic double lurking like him, unarmed
Who picks up more than hares: the cockchafers that come and go
When the terrier appears, the flies on the little one's eyes
And the brook beneath the sleeping grass. He doesn't see things any more
He sees what populates their shadows, earth's sub-proletariat
Smoke heavier than air
That lingering protects the Hebrews' houses.
It keeps predators away, the masters who can only make out
Upright bodies, clear high voices
Because that's their nature. They recognize murmurings
That rise but not those that drop
Nor the theoretical wake left by events
Which neither desire nor deserve to be remembered.
— There's nothing harder than locating the source
Of a sound, resonance aside
And what can you say about a mental wave
Clouded by neighboring frequencies? What follows?
No, the remainder of a remainder, vague relatedness
No longer interests most people, the last lines were muffled
By the springs of the fold-down chairs, drop by drop the room
Emptied out into darkness leaving only those
Held back by a personal grief hoping for
An encore: eternal widows of eternal husbands.
But you don't encore machines. One day on the phone
The invisible interlocutor will hold good, it won't be

Like in bad films when you see
The actor counting the suspension points in the script
He's reciting to a void. Here the voice will be there
Rolled tight into an ear a sound band ready to reply
To all your questions but quite right its responses
All foreseeable. That's what you expect
When a man dies. We'll have to make do
Without the main document no one knew about
When he was alive but that's missing in the archives
And the wire-tapping systems we forgot to unplug
Will sing on loop. — Luckily I can give you back
Your shaded sentences. It's not a very enticing proposition but you'll
Turn it to your advantage or you won't and either way
It will be perfect perfect very good very good.

HEAD DEEP IN THE WHITE STUFF

Something very simple
And another just as simple
Two very distant points fuse
Or not, everything continues still
To unfold in time you need an impressive reserve
Of faults
Uncertainty, fatal
Uncertainty.

— What do you mean exactly? — Exactly
That, yes, and that too. Something very simple
And another just as simple. If you take them together, together
They'll form quite a coherent image I think
A bit off-key perhaps but the real problem
Is elsewhere. It comes from the ban on saying everything
All at once. The following sentence in the interview
Replaces the preceding one and one alone isn't enough. Simple isn't it?
— Yes and no. Usually I read each shot of the film
With its subtitle. I know where I am and I advance.
You when you speak sound slangy. Memory is constrained
To acrobatics in real time. Tiring. And frustrating. Here's X
And Y. — Do they know each other? — Yes and how:
They're together. A ridge suddenly slips beneath the soles of your shoes
Earthquake crevice
It splits the whole map of your relationships
Two very distant points fuse. You are, yourself
In the hollow of the wave caught in the enjambement
One foot on each side of the temporal frontier

Hostage of the gangster or the cop
That he shouldn't meet at the corner of the road.
Short range. And now?
Everything should stop. Fear has suspended the scene
It actualizes the instant. Overturned coffee pot.
Burnt leg. A nightmare. Stop. I'm going to wake up.
Or not, everything keeps going on
And on. Got it? Or perhaps you're a translator:
Where it comes from where it's going isn't your business
Which involves substituting certain signs for others
In a long sequence. If it was inscribed
On the rotors of the Enigma code
You'd make them turn as though on the announcement board
In an airport. Anyhow your life's work
Would fit on a disk the size of an ashtray.
OK? Want any more?
OK. Look out the window.
Mountain one. Mountain two. Mountain three.
Until the seventh with only the crown visible
Covered with snow: mousse. There you are.
To unfold in time you need an impressive reserve
Of faults, of those lines that squeeze so many figures
Into each painting. The face of the young girl
In a drape in the middle will only be perfect when disfigured by
A fly. Then we'll love her, long to hold out
Our hand to stir the air, so that something happens at last
To the sound of Velcro.
Bitten nails, spittle, blemishes, ankles, mistakes, rips

Small barbs attach pretty things
On time. These mountains offer no practical route
No *clues:* no cluse. They tire me, frustrate me
And I'd like to unfold them, reduce them to dimension
One of the course — lets be reasonable, say one and a half
A fractal line. I try to draw
But lack ambiguity. Not the sfumato, a pathetic ruse
— Uncertainty, fatal
Uncertainty. — So you're trying to regain
That sensation of almost (almost
Being the term designating the greatest of small dangers)
In words? You go out, put your shoes on
To wallow feet deep in powder snow
Often tripping up on the object
The little pile. And you have to start over straightaway
When you fall, said the monitor. She added:
And what's more I'm right. That more troubles you. And if
She made you circle from mountain plain to mountain plain
On a slope eroded by ground water
That collapses in one night in a dull gurgling of mud
Spitting out trees and telegraph poles
Like small bones and you like the blind dervish
Of blind man's bluff to abandon you
At the top of a black slope in the mist? Stop.
You're back in the dream and it isn't a dream. — I got through
A few thousand kilometers in a couple of days
With you driving. And now?
Everything should stop, wake suddenly with

The apparition of cavaliers in uniforms from another century
In this avenue that doesn't sprout the Republican Guard
The way the American prairie sprouts Indians.
Or not, this comic epiphany was only a recompense
A snack for the journey. — We're not there yet?
— We're still going. Still flailing around beneath the powder snow
Knocking into all sorts of things that should be united.

AS A PLANE I WAS BORN TO A TRAM

Improvise
With constraints
To be completely free
To float
Depression, suck of air
But
They want to hear
The voice that gave orders during the decisive seconds
The thorniest question
What should have been desired?

Pick up the instrument
Play play
That's all, not without
Constraints against
Nature
Nothing more
Against our nature
Than flight flight
One third a push
Effort effort
Superhuman
Mechanical
Two thirds aspiration
Low pressure on the wings
Improvise
With constraints
Metallic welded
Fade-in on a backdrop

Of depression, that it draws
Upwards
Maybe may
Be quite free
Master master
Of machines
And able in everyway
To want everything without
Knowing what
To want if
You want mediocre things
Error
Of parallax, the Earth
Never seen from a vertical point
Of view
Never
These fields this backdrop
Catatonic
Shot
To float gas
Cut breath
Of a wind
Instrument, motifs, to play
Around with motifs clichés
To glide from there
Comes this emptiness came
These fade-ins lost
Lost how, illness

Infantile mortal
Called
Depression called
Feared
Condition
Of flight condition
Of abandon, there will be
Some logic in all that
Exchange of energy
Pushed against
Depression suck of air
It would be
Nice but no
Falling debris
Brisk wing strokes
Interlinked
Trace ʻ*u*ʼs
U
Of the ʻ*u*ʼs, the last
U is a
Half-*u*.

— I wanted to be a jazz musician aviator
Get up in the morning and play and fly
Or better: saxophone plane, reeds helixes
A toy of the air that's the closest
To obfuscating mental emptiness. To play
With constraints learned or invented.
Easy. But the improvisation, the flight
Doesn't leave the traces you think, the recording
Of information in the black box won't satisfy
The investigators after the crash, they want to hear
The voice that gave orders in the decisive seconds:
The tone, the tone. What happened, the moment
Of the mad decision, the emission of sound
Lost in advance shows nothing, its pleasure
Exaggerates desire and kills it in the bud. However
That abandon should have produced great things
Shouldn't it? That was the plan. Depression
Regains as they say the upper hand
(And it's no longer the one that draws upwards above the wings)
Because the improvised gesture sovereign within its reaches
Hasn't settled the thorniest question
The one a tram never poses the conductor
Between the rails and the electric cable,
That the investigators confused with that of motives
And the mechanics with that of operations:
What should have been desired? — It's the childhood sickness
Answer for nothing but ask trick questions absorbed
By tasks whose rules it changes without warning
Or infinitely sad. Lets start again from the beginning.

44

WHITE HIGH

A retarded passer-by
You notice that the schedule
Seems covered
With fingerprints
The bottleneck of practical thoughts
Is blocked. Something
Must escape these revolutions
Someone like him
In this stretch of extreme present.

Moving as an amnesiac he spends
Every day in the corner rarely
In the same street. His armpits itch like empty wallets.
It's a hole in the image
The idea of his soul denuded
Of a bit of de-pigmented skin, his skin
Of diaphanous russet, a second
Of joyful absence.
Nothing disturbing, the sun keeps
The table screwed to the floor
And the day within its benevolent grasp
— The sun. A retarded passer-by probably
Or someone prematurely aged from recognizing
Someone himself:
More is needed to disrupt the shots
To carry him over the now incredible fluidity
Of the dream of the waking person watching him.
What's more the danger comes from elsewhere
From dreams and fluid shots

Precisely, when you notice that the schedule of pleasures
Appears covered with the horse-shoe traces
Of fingerprints.
Have the minute thieves
Dropped by? — They're good, you know:
You open your program one fine day, everything's fine
Until you try to access some application and then
No response
A ridiculous dead-end
Where there had been an information highway.
You note the clues a little later:
They're going to sell on memory sticks
With indistinguishable content
While the insurance man in a red suit (very reassuring)
Points out that immobile furniture (strange notion)
Isn't covered. What hurts
Isn't so much the loss as its opposite, say the victims
— Violated intimacy, disorder, in short the excess
Of goods that are the same. — So the once
Exciting projects appear trampled
By someone else and the miniscule goals you set
Administrated hour after hour like an aphrodisiac
Achieved a priori.
Hypermenia? The intruder
It's him it's me the drudge
In a hurry to get rid — of what?
— Of the verbal reflection, the overload when he swings round
Too early. The sun
Turning hardens the corner. Ice forms.

And the guys are afraid to bore you. They shouldn't be.
The air has simply pushed the landscape back
Behind its opaque varnish.
The hangman's knot of practical thoughts
And acts necessary for what follows
At the service of an out of date desire
That no one saw building up at the bottom of the sink
It's stuck. Something
Must escape these solar revolutions. Something
Must dig a hole, refuse to submit to the tides
The aggravating dialectic of fluid and solid.
Something or someone on a white high.
— I've heard that expression. I don't know what it means.
A powder-based psychotrope? A western sport?
Reserve figuring on a dark image?
Someone like him pale and serious
Who takes short steps, tries to find his way
Free from all memory and all fault of memory
Under the shock, under the effect of some gymnastic or drug
That blocks his brain effacing all information
— An enviable fate, don't you think?
— For a few seconds, yes
But that would be quite enough because you'd settle into them
As into country life for life in a whitewashed
Bunker converted into an asylum
On the bank of a dead limb: a whole existence
In this stretch of extreme present
With its pylons, lock gates, rails, refinery,
Of extreme absence with its wasteland and calm water.

A NUDE

The thing
Touch it
To disturb
Form.

To ascertain the existence of
The thing there
Thing — essential —
Seen every day
Always in a frenzy
Consciousness of time reduced
To arrow point
Space reduced
To a corner
Bottom of a tightly gathered bag
Touch it
Cautiously afraid
Of wakening its
Painful nudity of
Crumpling it of
Flattening it out but ever so
Excitable mollusc
Blind when
Retracting expanding
So you also want to disturb
Form
Extraordinarily profuse
Slight

48

Of a crest
That disappears passes
Into another passing on
The energy of the folding
In waves
Red holà oh
My God to kiss
The face without eyes the eye
Without a face?

SUBTLE MUSIC

Call it part of the furnishings
Or music of the brain
The dream
Would be
To be the inconsequential accompaniment
To your half-sleep
Adjusting contours and seams
To the atmospheric feeling.

Liquid, with no clear beginning: a rising in the pipes
In the immaculate enamel toilet bowls, the taps
Polished up by the words 'dub,' 'tub,' 'plumb'
Rubber balls bouncing off each other.
Careful it's not a metaphor
You really hear it from a distance
And it's joyful, I promise, almost completely
Joyful. Call it part of the furnishings
Ambient floating trip-hop
Or music of the brain even
If you like don't listen to it too closely
To smooth out the worrying bumps
In the background, ventilators of reanimation
Groans and ritornellos of an old man a cappella
Defused by the dumb hammering
Or very brief cries
With neither the attack nor the weary bypassing
Of pain. The dream
Would be not to produce as I do

Nor to listen like you — because those allergic
To Muzak stuck in the lift
With no window nor clairvoyants to say
If they're on the twenty fifth floor or three levels below ground
Die in dreadful agony —
But to be, yes
To be the inconsequential accompaniment
To your half-sleep in which fall
Fall and flow oscillating lightly
Words words
Beneath the surface that reflects nothing.
Strange: the sounds that furnish
Their presence that now seems
Disarming is their weakness.
They form a precocious memory, a one-way dialogue
With no authority borne however
By the side that carries it. Where do they go?
That's the mystery of lighters:
We've accepted the idea that they disappear magically
So why do none of them ever reappear?
I think that the rotation of the grind
Transforms them into heat
I mean literally
Because used literally words
Consume each other completely for good
Each time. Oh cigarettes
Oh black coffee, oh entropy!
Am I talking nonsense? Very well

I'm talking nonsense to calm us
Adjusting the contours and seams
Of the two-backed beast. Sweet
Very sweet. — And great music
And art then, Jean-Noël? Ah I love it.
I too see stars
When I blow my nose
But we cling each day
To the atmospheric feeling too cowardly
To fix ambition to edify
The opaqueness and nebulousness of a truth, we cling to even
More than to whatever it is, so much the worse for it, so much the worse
For great good, for great beauty. And sweetness
Doesn't filter through small poetry
Couplet-chorus from Rock FM
But from a still humbler mouth
Air-con that whispers and ambient sounds:
Don't listen out for me, don't find me.

THE FIANCÉS

Love is a special effect
The thing is that there's no magic spell
The charm
Is mechanical
Then
The imp
Who stole for you
Will have to be made.

Love is a special effect
Said the thief from Baghdad speaking as a connoisseur.
From his aisle — all the trajectories within the bared angle
Of a poor art — he obtained
The rarest coins using strings
Hooks and diversions: white lies.
But he kept nothing for himself strangely
Intact and bare-chinned — a child. He amused you
Too in a variation when it's an illiterate thief
Who marries the beggar become king
And in another he's a barber. Such a shame
That he pinned the beauty down on his flying carpet
Leaving you to deal with the victory
After the credits. The first trick he taught you:
The apparition of the man in the water
Over which the woman leans — called 'the mixed mirror'
(The man lies on a branch behind the woman
Success guaranteed.) And if you'd prefer
Scripts with photos there was also:

Him 'I've gone blind, guide me'
Her 'They're forcing me to marry a bad man'
And 'I'll give you up to save your life'.
The thing is that there's no magic spell
A complicit dimmer has diffused the blue
Light around the blue mosque, shoe-shiners have passed
Over the pavement on the terrace broad as a stadium
At the time of your date, the scene was entitled
Summer dusk. The philtres were made of
Natural plant extracts, a pleonasm bittersweet as
A kiss. Yes that works by itself —
What's a film if not a machine room
The jewel of the Sultan of Basra's collection
Italian-style toy theater where
Miniature dancers turn? We wanted to surpass it
Proposing the kit for a white wooden horse
That trots over the clouds when you turn the key
But there was magic mixed in and contrary to what you'd expect
That breaks the charm, you know, the charm
Is mechanical. Visible threads
A giant metallic spider, a halo
Around the giant genie standing out against the shadow
Fulfil your wishes. Since your engagement
The world filmed from its most flattering
Angle is called Orient. Up above
The deceitful omissions of your guardian angel
Are hollowed out by the zoom before a slide-shot back
Where? Where? The promise of a

Happy end clear-cut in the contract
Will convert the reality debit
Into credit using the detour of a strophe
On payday, won't it?
— Don't insist on the question, the more you ask for the more
You reduce your chances. You only need to know
That it turns on quite a simple artifice.
Decide once and for all where you want the camera
And keep your eye glued to the peephole, letting the little
Special effects mastermind work. Then, then
You'll have to do everything yourselves, reckon that
You'll no longer have anyone's gaze to guide you
Through the ruby eye of the goddess — what
Was her name again? — A makeshift religion
For superstitious lovers. The imp
Who stole for you when treacherous viziers
Kept you apart, you must do it, send him home
By plane and reign over your fiscal paradise
Without the film-crew, the contrasts, the mist that
Assisted your affairs. — A child's game? Well then
Bring me a child. — He's on his way, Sire.

A DEFENSE OF POETRY

That happens
Here
Between the acute sensation and the latent feeling
Entering you
Troubled the old game of both soul
And landscape
So I really need you if I'm to advance.

What joy to see you walking over
My territory, exchanging a few
Insignificant words in passing with the garden
Gnomes. Human figures had become silent
In the constructed part of the domain
On the boundary an aged man barely held
Anyone's attention as he cut the end off a banana
Bearing a bar-code with a Swiss penknife.
Yes, from the first sensation
The visible side announces the color
The code of the day: the nature
Of its link with what's hidden. That happens
Here, not in the 'un-said'
But between the views of the moment
Of the area all completely accurate
And what they cover up is what must be said.
A hydraulic jack supports the gallery
I lean on it, I test its resistance
On each line. Each line measures
The distance between the décor

56

The record set up and it's shadow
Inventory you lay down in writing —
Between the acute sensation and the latent feeling, enters
Between. But this capricious proportion that rules
My unhealthy flow, rhythms it, gets it going
Had frozen in the usual places. A whole area
Won over by the desert and its cold nights
And its mad-wind-that-no-one-listens-to-expecting-to-get-away-with-it.
The same set-up: the gaze of regulars who avoid each other
Preferring to hand back the change of words in profile
Walls and floor polished darkly by daydreams
For daydreams, sketches rehearsed a thousand times
Before an audience of chairs. Entering you
Troubled the old game of both soul
And landscape. The air you displace when you walk
Has re-swollen the card figures that belong here.
— That leaves us with quite a lot of images
Doesn't it? What was last night's T.V. drama about?
I didn't even get if it was a docudrama
Or something else. — Yes, everything's getting muddled up this morning
Or rather juxtaposed, one view bang another
Unequal doses of sun, passers-by, cars, cement
That nothing links except the analogy whose logic
Vanishes into the next vision. — I hope at least
That when sewing them together you understand more clearly
What they're hiding in your poor little head.
— In two words I call that the sentimental
So I really need you if I'm to advance

From one comparison to the other ironically
Naively in this indirect light
This 'reality' that quotes itself
And moves away. Because behind it, far behind
Realism and imagination stand around
In a mortal docudrama. — That's all?
— That's all, I've said too much, it's your fault.
Now let's change terrace
Let's look for silence but outside.

OTHER METHODS

When
Sunday
Gets you down
Do the Hausa
The Aka
The Jivaro

When the iron shutters
Fall and people
Get that floury look
Like fillets of whiting, Sunday
Gets you down you say
You'll never do anything

        Then
Do the Hausa that mimics the horn-bill
Stuck in the bulrushes two three leaves
On the head for the tail
Raised arm bent hand
Fingers folded into a beak the cry
Completes the mouth
Pursed-lipped

        Do
The Aka baby pygmy
Lulled at the entrance to the hut
Early in the morning very early
By the yodel his mother still young
And beautiful hums low

Very low because she's still half-asleep
Hopes you'll leave her another hour
And by her cousin still young and beautiful
Also with beautiful breasts in
Counterpoint redoubtable
Counterpoint you open an eye
Ouhou ouhou ouhou
You turn over in the odour
Of last night's fire

                                        Do
The Jivaro that grates
Its creeper packaging the turnings
Spits makes the red liquid
Run cooks it dips
Its arrow in the jam
Takes off in a sigh no
One saw it no one saw
The bird fall and you
You are like it in the forest
State Sunday
Gone gone
With your prey your feathered phrase.

GASOMETER

A moribund memory
A cylindrical cage
Air belonging to the past
Mourning
Is these days terrifyingly brief
But fiction, constructing
The so un-monumental monument
Of the day
Well in that case.

It might as well not work
The gasometer by the river, that point
Of connection, a memory too moribund
To have an odour, we could only see
The summit from a distance and from nearby not
Much like cathedrals at the time
Of cathedrals, it was always night
And now it's in the night of time
— What your short-wicked memory sets off
Funfair before we've settled on our chairs
To see it, everything you insist
On constructing and not without talent alas
Suffering from a lack of materials: too soft
Or too fragile — balls of rice
Two mouthfuls connected by a thread of
Melted cheese called themselves telephones
And the gasometer a cylindrical cage
Made up of wide metal links that was
Air belonging to the past with

61

Its kids and stealthy fog
Risen low from the invisible river
And the pizzerias of the past shut
It sums it up in its shaky inconsistent
Way, a more than precarious
Erection – when the phone rang
In the middle of the night dreams veered
Towards two classics: obscene provocation
Death announced but there was no
Voice just a mechanical snoring
As though a door had opened
On the vacant network, sound of the extinction
Of sounds, bottom of a shell – what is it
That makes the jingle of
This furious year inaudible, for example
Hüsker Dü? – the violence was the
Violence of the present quite simply
You must learn a new programming
Language it seems – already?
– You mean again? – yes, what's difficult
Isn't mourning, mourning
Is these days terrifyingly brief
The eyes of the building opposite shade themselves
– As well as possible – then we get back to following
The news but fiction, constructing
The so un-monumental monument
Of the day, words deliberately
Banal, rhythms wobbly, well in that case

No bonus in sight, no harmony
No unity, no perenity
It's counting more or less to ten on the fingers
Of an armless man, cutting a master copy in a gas
With an upholsterer's tape measure, that's it.

A bolster as long as a life
Stuffed with archives
We'll take turns
Snoring as hard as monks pray
But careful
The slower you go, the harder it is
To stop.

You can't imagine this place
Without someone sleeping in it.
You need a bolster as long as a life
With the heat and odor
Of flesh in the summer when air
Softly displaces two buttocks on
A bench, salts and sweetens breath.
It's stuffed with archives this bolster
Nourishment for dreams that are memory
Relieved. We'll take turns
For the opposite of guard duty
Snoring as hard as monks pray
Standing in for all those staying up
So brave and they'll be happy
To tiptoe
To whisper, their crazy whisperings
Will soothe us. Of course the water weighs down
Our clothes, you can't say
It gets hotter hour after hour, and then
We chomped through a lot on the beach

Filling our earthworm's stomachs –
All the sand piled up behind! But the camera's
As good as new, a girl
Behind the window on the other side of the courtyard
Wriggles as she dries the dishes
In deathly silence – yes that's how
I dance. The festive period is over
Good riddance, that of fine dinners
Isn't coming thank God. – I'd like to be
As old, as lively as a reptile's eye
And recognize the same face everywhere
The most expansive, the most closed
The youngest, the most particular, the face
Of Maria Schell, the one that in a marvellously
Soporific film pronounces
…but the clouds. It'll come:
What could stand in the way of
Such a minuscule ambition? the fear
Of missing something? confirmed
Beyond our hopes. Visiting time
Goes quickly on this metallic multifunctional bed
Where you play with the pulleys to keep time
While the women in white cry
'Mambo!' and every cancellation
Is a blessing. But careful.
That funny customer, that drunk admit it
That hopeless case who mumbles prayers
Believing he's speaking of love, your secret mentor

65

Isn't much help because he's sleeping
With his eyes open. Better to share the work
Take a secretary to forget
The same way businessmen buy themselves
Joggers. The working population will pay
Someone like you not to do
What you don't do so well, and you
You'll pay a socialite who'll tell you everything
While paying a careerist.
From hand to hand a symbolic coin will pass
At the speed of light, the sun
Will rise, fall and
Rise again within a minute. What do think about that?
– Too much commotion. I prefer the obese clouds
The transformation of the past into downy feathers
And alarms go off too early
To be taken literally. Please
Don't see it as reticence or laziness.
Swimming eventually thickens the water
The slower you go, the harder it is
To stop, the difference
Becomes too minute, the task
– To stay there on the cusp
Eyelids almost shut –
Exhausting and grandiose as strange
As that may seem. How to catch up with
The tortoise of sleep, seize
The toppled instant? – See you tomorrow

You said yesterday: *to-morrow*, and once again
A word carried us over the line.

AT LEAST ONCE A DAY

Strange
That the mechanism carries it off
With less efficiency
Unless
There's a plot involved
Ah
The swell rises again, a miracle
The pretty jumping jacks start drumming again.

For our species of robot
A word incites an anecdote
Just one, fallen
In the public domain.
Small numbers follow each other
Like dishes, we believe in it
As long as there's no collision.
We speak in second gear
Of old stories and new
Constructions, we remember things
Well up to last year
But as for this memory here and now
That gives collective robots consciousness
Nothing. Anyway
The springs relax
Movements segment
Dialogues dry out
Still.
Well. –
Well, it's strange

That the mechanism carries it off
With less efficiency contrary
To what's believed, that a photo of a chimpanzee
Now decorates the desk of the man who taught us philosophy
Re-named psychology of cognition
And that the chances of friendly
Exchange, of changes in the line-up
Of circulation of people and goods
Should be cancelled out one after the other
With no one batting an eyelid. Strange
Such blindness. Unless
There's a plot involved? The neighbors
Faces are intact except for the snarl
They reserved for their mirrors
Which now masks them
Stars of a forgotten film
(*The List of Adrian Messenger*) one by one
Replaced by the passengers
Of the night meteor
Body snatchers
Or the village's damned
Los-Angelic invaders. –
Only a few fragments of an
Unknown fallen metal
That has the marks, the glint of pure present
Prove we haven't been dreaming. The car
They exhibit pierced
By the bolide at the museum's door

Is far too negative an indication. Because everything
May have changed surreptitiously
Except the never-ending question
Posed by the confused spectator boring us to death
– What happened? So when will the head of the welcome party
Announce it with a sinister grimace?
– There have been changes.
Paranoia simply inverses
Certain arrows along the way
So that the landslides
The new buildings, the expansion of the wasteland
And the season that render the surroundings un-recognizable
Instead of signalling an absurd power of inertia
Seem destined for you. – Alas
The facts are much more simple
And chaotic. Each drop followed its path
To the end. The automation
Of the translations has finally stabilized
Meaning in an opaque newspeak. People
Mingled, the more they've
Felt un-desired the more they render themselves
Undesirable. Each one
Steered like a car parallel parks
Won't budge now. – Well.
There's a moment like that.
Every day the timetable changes
You never see it coming.
– And another when you push the packaging

70

With a straw where indicated: ah
The swell rises again, a miracle
The pretty jumping jacks start drumming again
Sure that today will be their day
That we'll give them life for good this time
And who'll have the heart to let them down?
– You? The last on the preceding list
And the first on the next
Always ready for your turn
On the crank or the carousel? Come on
Act tough like the rest of them; you must
Make your evening prayer in the evening, your morning prayer
In the morning. Say the opposite.

FAY WRAY MEETS BUSTER BROWN

The stock of incarnations
Is excessive
Emotions have their forms
In the cinema
Something
So calming
About you
We declared peace
In clean-cut frames.

The stock of incarnations
Is overflowing. The reflections stream
Along the bottom line
Of the pyramid of glasses.
Instead of a picked button-holed
Carnation several are
Growing. – When you no longer control anything
You pick out an object, a face
In the marriage agency's album
For each fragment of signification
And here is the rebus-portrait.
It's a real bouquet: a shot
With Fay Wray's eyes
The echo of water lapping
In a covered swimming pool
Deserted = Fear.
Other emotions have their preferred forms too
Mainly available in the cinema
Increasing editable platitude.

They're made for
The meccano of memory. Fay Wray
Whose body still lives could be
Resumed by her face itself resumed by her eyes
Was only a name for 'afraid'
The inverse shot of a monster. So
A spectator unknown
To the others and to himself
Arranges his hair by manipulating his shadow
On the ground. – There is something
So calming in this flattening
Out and from a distance
When you think about it if you're mad enough
To think about it: everything is there
Already installed, fear
Simply being the most intense
Passion sold to order. – As
You flicked through the dictionary of actors
Your bible in which possible conflicts
Facile expressions have flourished once and
For ever, around you
We declared peace
By surprise, each fighter
Having covered the whole cycle
Of their metamorphoses in Switzerland.
Sides numerous as the spokes
Of a bicycle wheel didn't consult one another
In order to put the brakes on. We traders

Threw the dinner invitations in the pit
And secret agendas were placed on the table.
We exchanged incredulous glances
Now hearing nothing but a spade
Scraping the cement a few floors down:
The burying of arms or perhaps
The beginning of a new worksite.
– Anyhow, the multilateral withdrawal
Of forces is only momentary. You knock into
Something else behind, shielding yourself from the danger
Which involves taking everything too much to heart as they say
You'll fall over backwards. A desire
That wasn't on the list will open something
Deeper. – I know, the scars will look like
Beauty spots next to
The next wound. Until then
Let's pretend to contemplate the world
OK? And take resolutions
Of pure form. After the fear of the counter-attack
Before the re-offensive, a little cunning:
Buster Brown has been punished
He writes on a huge poster
That he repents but he thinks he's right
And mocks his parents' justice.
It's the last panel at the bottom of the page. On the next
Things will be worse. – So acts and the marks they leave
On the protagonists' skin
Are all shown in colour or in black

In clean-cut frames
Then stocked at a constant temperature
Accessible to all not even for the edification
Of new arrivals – for use
Quite simply. They'll draw
Like you from the stream of images
Abstract bits of smalt
With which they'll compose the silhouette
Of the monstrous feeling that pulls
In both directions, the feeling
Will explode right there in this shape
Too forcefully offered
For metaphor.
But there will be a moment of peace, a quasi-
Story you make up before sleeping
In order to sleep and that the night
Will dislocate. – And then? – And then
The reserves will seem more abundant
The vegetation even denser
And the agitation, having once been incarnated
In our chatty playlets, intenser.

WHAT WAS IT

Let it end
This day
Fossilized in the egg
Or
To redo
The paint
An odor
Of life
Hop
Gone
Ah damned
Elegance

Ah to hurtle down with
This clear noise of spokes
The road that bears
A name its very own name
Stolen from the great man
The grade meets
The grade increases
The speed of the chestnut trees
In rows and clusters of
White or red flowers cling
To a precious thread for
It doesn't last, when it
Counts

      Let it end
Razed close razed
Fresh by the air

This day free-
Wheeling this turn
Of the dial that stops
In a foetal
Position everything
Fossilized in the egg
Of a diplodocus yes
So I said

        Beautiful
Says the mouth yawning
At the gnats
It drinks
The mouth, speaking while breathing in
Things the eyes fixed
On the asphalt hardly see
At all

        Let's admit
If we have to that the spring-like
Effect such
Clarity doesn't
Last but to stop it break it there
Halfway, the traffic light
Now green
And the reaction would be
Just a stupid accident, distracted
Suddenly

Why not

      Or
To redo
The next day in other words
Today with no migraine
The paintwork
Heaven
That no one will ever
Take back from you
Because you gave it
Exhaled it as soon as
Inspired

      An odor
Follows common
As an insect, poor
Sample
Of life stings and then at last
Touch and hop
Gone

      In order for
It to be good
You must hear it said but
Dilemma
Above all
Not to ask

If it was good

    Afterwards
Don't force it the slope's
Enough the wind
Loosens the lots
Bunches, mistletoe and straw
Rolled up in hoops
Bicycle wheels you're pretending
To manipulate

    A clown
Slipping after an onlooker he imitates
To perfection seems
To climb on his back
Or a Chinese strategist
That melds with the other
Invisible side
It's so you
And me

    That
Vanishes and leaves
An Easter egg
But where in my memory
Ah damned
Elegance, it'll be wonderful
Won't it?

ADVENTURES IN THE TROPICS

An estuary, you ascend it
As you turn back time
Time counted
Will expand
But
To obtain one minute of this stay
You had to trace four thousand drawings on a calque.

The story remains a little confused.
An old seadog mumbles
On the bridge of a ship bound for the large
That draws away from the port by night
Very slowly. You can hardly make out
His silhouette and nothing of
Those listening to him, unless they're sleeping.
No luck: he's the narrator.
He creates sentences
Descriptions, comparisons, explanations
With remnants of dreams. He aims
For truthfulness and clarity but it's the effort
That attracts the most attention
As with tightrope-walkers. Is it
That someone told him of the curse unleashed
On certain fantastic vessels
And secondary elaboration?
– There was, he said, at the end
Of this stormy crossing
(I'll come back to it) a house.

Let's glance ahead for to get to this house
You ascend an estuary
A bit as you turn back time. So
Just as you settle in you notice
That you've lived there before – that's how in fact
You recognize it (wonderful retrospective
Recompense!). – As for the listeners
You now see the whites of their eyes
Lifted skywards. Then follow pictures
Of exotic edens, life on land as
Sailors imagine it. Time above all
Time counted but suspended at sea
Will blossom like a floating flower
Planted at last. But this story
Of the estuary and the needles turning the wrong way
Proves that he hardly understands the notion,
Unconscious. It's not by chance
That he passed over the details. He's old
He's drunk, he hopes no one will want to
Needle him about the unfortunate encounters
And harsh trials he's left out.
For to obtain one minute of this stay in such a distant place
You had to trace four thousand drawings onto calque
And photograph them while colouring the film
By hand. Why not? if it's about offering
The spectators the experience of their life
The densest, most scribbled over and gracious
Lapse of time there's been

As Windsor MacCay did in 1911
To take up an alcoholic's challenge.
But to found the future – our future –
On this sort of bet, such dissymmetry
– No. We should love obstacles
Not look too closely at destinations
If we want to last in this line of work.
Instead: recount adventures in the tropics
Before this, well, doubtful ending: shipwrecks?
Sea monsters? cannibalism? – Perfect.
That will keep us awake until we're out at sea.

BLAME IT ON THE HEAT, I

Faster
Cut the silence
A funnel forces throats open
It concerns ballistics
Presence of mind with the return
Of the ball with a certain twist
Now just
Speak
Faster than their shadow.

Faster
And nonchalantly please
Cut the silence that's cosmetic
Whale fat
To hell with repetitive songs old refrains
That stick, they slam
The shutters, open with an explosion
Cocktail of gas and rainwater
That staves off thirst, sharpens it
To force down the chitchat
Of all times and customs, pills
Gilded to perfection come thick and fast
A funnel forces throats open, divine
Compression of data unconstrained
By optical fibres, oh bric-a-brac
Devalued coins already
Old but not yet antique
Demagnetized coupons you
Then attain the sublime equality

Of the photocopier, sheen
Of chemical light over Earth
Lubricated at last like
The bottom of the developing tank, the more hostile
Reminiscences are all the readier they're
Taken together when it's time to chat
With happiness that won't be
Denied if it draws the carpet
As we suspected from beneath the feet
Of the supervising authorities
Don't look now
Don't lose sight of the Morse
On the asphalt, it concerns ballistics
Neck supple bent forward
Presence of mind with the return
Of the ball with a certain twist
Parabolic, jaculatory
Casualness and a wake of cartridges
Warm as fresh droppings go
Quietly they bombarded you
With slogans, with de-labelled words
The instrument of death, ingredients
Present in the neighbor's store-room
Good thinking, now just
Send it back unpinned, speak
Faster than their shadow, that ruins
The atmosphere, these days
It's hospital silence

They're filming the millionth sequel
Of *The Prisoner*, after a hundred and twenty
Beats you've got the right to lyricism
Both moral and sentimental, transmitted
With the Doppler sound wave
Listen it's started
Leaving a scalding signature.

NOT A TRANSACTION

That's how debt works
A loser. Losing
There, they're all free as air
In briefs and silent
I'd like to change sides
To have neither creditors nor debtors
Broaden the view
And profit from the elasticity – modest
But real of the instant.

One minute was enough and the payer
No longer recognized the face
Of the buyer. – You yourself, says the cashier.
Cantankerous he won't be held accountable for anything, berates himself.
– I'm reimbursing your arrears indefinitely.
Where were you when the meter was turning?
Who were you drinking with? – But what do the loans matter
Because from another point of view thanks to this fickleness
Each hour becomes an island with
Its exotic ritual, its barter of shells
A stock that the tide will renew
And its unexpected sacrifices defying the reason
Of White Men. Bad faith was necessary
For justice to be reclaimed when you sense
The expected going up in smoke
With the daily pyre lit by the sun
Looked at through a magnifying glass. So it's more
A fire of joy, then? – He's complaining of something else
The moaner: of not being as prodigal

As the weather, of not opening the port-holes
Wide enough to measure the wind, drawing down
The allied currents. A rescue generator
Then takes over, maintaining the illusion
Of new forces by recycling the ashes.
That's how debt works, always the same
Lack of nobility. A loser. Losing twice over
Something the figures keep quiet. – What? – Nothing:
The event consumed on site. A card reads:
As we speak, elsewhere… A dining couple
Talk in the third person and in narrative present
Of you or even more bizarrely
Not of you. There, they're all free, not one
Holds you back, at the moment. As
You manoeuvred a rather fictitious little boat
Using guess-work as though it was a galley
And you were forced to take command over
One hundred and fifty of your alter egos, galley slaves,
Freedivers, filmed
By the second unit you knew nothing about
And whose shots will be edited behind your back
Because you can't have the *final cut* of this story,
Make holes in the sides to let the water in.
See if they're free as air in briefs and silent
And you quite safe, babbling. Wounded under water
They bleed like people smoke, it's not blood
It's red. So? No regrets?
– Actually yes. I'd like to change sides, with them

Against me: torpedo-boat sniper.
To have neither creditors nor debtors nor ambition
Nor... – Regrets? Lost. Another
Resentful response.
Such daydreams aren't meant to escape the circle of
Usury. You wake after the battle
On a sea of old oil in which half-
Empty glasses carrying half-
Smoked cigarettes float as far as you can see. It's not too late
To make peace with yourself as they say
Without concessions for an increase
Of capital, of life. Broaden the view
By twirling it in mid-air like a pizza base
And profit from the modest but real elasticity
Of the instant. A little further
Forward, a little further
Back, yes, there we are.
A longer sentence, with more ramifications
Taken in at a glance. Tiny island illuminated
From behind by the sun, in front another
Shadowed by a mini-cloud. The tension
Of the thread they had to hold taught between them
Keeps things above water, occupies you completely
And saves you of course from settling debts whether old
Or new. – Yes, I stick close to
An archipelago sometimes that records everything all
The time. Coded exchanges
Potlatches, hagglings and chatter

Make up the spectacle
On the shore. If from out at sea you can see
Several simultaneous small-scale ceremonies
I can no longer make out – coasting along freely –
A single transaction. Thank you
For your advice. Here: with eyes screwed shut
And a stupid smile, I nod.

BLAME IT ON THE HEAT, 2

To escape with you
From the circuit
Restrict the traffic
The communication
The cultural exchange
Of that lot the bookmakers
Who sell and buy language.

Would that I could escape with you
From the commercial circuit
They'd only have time to say
Hats off
Flag down red card
And it would be the wall
In Daytona in the dust
Heat swelling the foot
On the accelerator
Summer shut up shop
Restrict traffic to the ring roads
Communication to answering machines
God is it possible
When oxygen has its sponsor
Due to outstanding payments
Brain poorly irrigated I do
A headstand
A somersault
Over the bale of hay
Stop moving

Hold fast without dividends
In a dignified pose
As though separating
The grain from the chuck
But it's the ergot of the wheat
The cultural exchange
In clinking change
Before it's back to work
We'll have to burn
The whole harvest I'm afraid and
A craving
Regarding my disdain
Or to the shame of that lot
The bookmakers
In the stands
Selling and buying language
It's a promise we'll no longer run
For the team farewell golden youth of the
Internet farewell
Gossip columnists
We'll remember you
From the taste when
We sick you up
Are they your bones
Laminated in the sheet metal
No, but you didn't say no
Soaked in champagne.

We find the appropriate position
Naïve artists of our sort
Consecrate their lives to minute adjustments
– And publicity, then? That's the thing
There's always some
Wagg family that exploits it to turn everything upside down.

And your convalescence? – Interrupted.
The puzzle was almost complete and the sheet almost smooth
When the door opened on Jolyon Wagg's
Tribe. – You'd forgotten your birthday!
– Everything'll have to be re-done now, yet again.
That's what happens with health, it's sensitive to publicity.
We find the appropriate position for the board and the iron
To smooth out the trapeze of white light
That reappears each morning, the appropriate position
For the chair in relation to the window
And the direction of the gaze along the connected rooms
So that 1. It incorporates the door-less rooms
In order to cross them and land in blue sky
And 2: It can assemble those cardboard bits
Of sky on the table always the hardest part
All a brutal blue. Admit
That it's not an easy job:
Naïve artists like us
Consecrate their lives to minute adjustments
To which no account does justice
Too dull and liable to proportion-based

Comedy. But that's how each of us
– Don't worry we're not numerous
I register lantern signals at dawn –
Works on their health in their little room.
– What a situation. – I know
You mustn't go shouting out about it
But don't forget the slogan: this concerns all of us!
And as for the health I'm talking about
The honour of the establishment is at stake.
– And publicity, then? That's the thing
It's not recommended. We limit it
To courtesy visits. Though there's always some
Wagg family that exploits it to turn everything upside down. Well
Sometimes we lug an exemplary case
To the amphitheatre, and make a saint & martyr of him
But a stand-in took his place at a moment's notice
In front of pretend spectators appointed the day before
Experts in multimedia communication like him:
His cast-off vows pass through modems
Persuading millions of small share-holders
That they've placed their money well, however
The real patient works miracles
At the back of a staff waiting room deserted by the interns
Who wouldn't miss the auto-celebration ceremony
For anything. He adds a chapter
To clinical pathology and at this stage
No-one's certain anymore whether to call it illness
Or mutation. – That reminds me

What exactly were you saying? Two things
In one? An allegory? – Quite the opposite
Like you I speak so as not to speak of this
Or that, so as never to have to reply
To those with things to say
Doctors or sales reps. I like stories
With no logic to them that ridicule
All vague desires for identification in advance.
This room chosen as you choose a side
Dug deep beneath the boards that mimic the universe
(Because according to them there's only one side
Clearly observable and instead of adversaries
Wagg spectators) well this room
Undergoes complete film-set treatment too
By default. We took the pictures off the walls
Which now seem to float, we turned off
The projectors leaving a single lamp in the shot
And when the actors play their roles for the first take
I say: perfect, start again with half the volume.
– Don't forget to burn the unwanted shots
To stop the editor adding bits
To flesh out the intrigue, as they say.
– No danger of that, it doesn't interest anyone,
It wasn't really meant for anything that banal home-movie
Just to get us on our feet by cleaning out our eyes
But when it comes to my health or yours nothing costs too much.

THE SHORTEST DISTANCE

Blurred close shots
The portrait
Isn't
Lifelike
Lower down
The substance
Of love
Puckers
Unnoticed.

Blurred close shots, the price
Of natural lighting
It's you so little
Like yourself

Bowled over, the pieces
Of this chess-set
Reel on the brink
Of day for I see you

From very nearby, the holes
That establish themselves
Beneath the words eyes nostrils mouth
I thought they'd give up

Wandering around, no
The portrait on a doily
Of open-worked paper
Eaten isn't

Spat, lifelike, within language
You're as unrecognizable
As anything as
You are, let's look

Lower at night
The vermilion substance
Of love lets you
Touch it but puckers

Unnoticed with
Track-ball clitoral
Orgasm the heart
Of a doe offered up

Steaming by the hunter
To Snow-White's mother
He couldn't
All the better, then

It's necessary to remake
The sacrifice, true
Though not quite on
Target the shot

Deviated it's my voice
Murmurings
Settle push back
The riverbank oh

Polder in progress oh principal
Of uncertainty the closer I get
It's strange the less
In focus you are

Sharp, my half-
Distance glasses
Off you float
I row.

FORMAL SELF SPEAK

I won't escape
The ridicule entailed by speaking to you absent
You said
Construction and lumps
Are the two most tenacious forms of reality
You were pitiless with those like you the best at translation
My dear friend
I would like to talk to you.

It's right here we spoke of construction and lumps
Sitting very straight on our fake leather chairs, barely touching
The formica table, using indirect sentences
And even if your brusque prudent wader's gestures
Re-positioned you even then in profile and very far back
In current memory, I won't escape
The ridicule entailed by speaking to you absent. – Let's start again:
What were you saying? – We think in terms of lumps. Labial
Like swallows' spit gastric time absorbs
Objects sucked in when the cover's open, glue
And bile combining, it filters them and breaks them down but
Sometimes stocks and agglutinates them. At a particular rhythm clots
And unexpected concretions form and resist
Even more easily as the great churn beats
With more fury. (Parentheses on planet formation
Or that of pancake batter.) – We think in terms of construction
Lines, angles, balance maintained firmly by the mind
Next to the building solid and sheltered from the suspect aspects
Of the site promised to disappear the day before
The inauguration. But what's been built threatens ruin

Before the termination of the works, in the domain of thought
The temporary is becoming incrusted, gaining disciples and creating
School programs. (Parentheses on the geometric method
Or pre-fabricated secondary schools.) – In such a way, in such a way that
Scaffolding and lumps however abstract they may appear
Are the most tenacious forms of reality.
I burst out laughing when one of the dumbfounded people at the table
Made a conciliatory remark. – Ha
You said with a challenging glance, it's insane!
Because you were pitiless with those like you the best at translation
Servants and future masters. – Our pedagogues are only interested
In capital, pure porn and they don't even go to the place for it
Poor things, you said. Be less prudish, less economical
And they get furious, ah, I perceive good tendencies
In one of the youngest recognizable from his extremely straight neck,
Conclave they piss each other off mutually
Full stops, mutations also speak of byways, residential flats
Complain of rheumatism while massaging in Tek
Theory and completely senile as a result of innuendo
Will soon have lost all ability to understand anyone else.
– It's still necessary to recognize the fact that, yes, they've since kept
Their promises the most mediocre though
You didn't follow that career to cut
Your wood that paid for the incunabula's binding
Nor write the third manifesto
Camp. – Because camp, you said in your Platonician
Perfecto, is neither a style nor the idea of a style
But the thought of that idea, elegance over taste

And it would go against it to write about it. – My dear friend
       I would like to talk to you
       Tenderness of the calf beneath its mother
       Crazy unforeseen breasts
       Deforming men's shirts
       Or other people's conjugal joy
Silly things that will amuse you despite that strength both uncommon
And common distancing you even further
Today when it pierces me with the hook of this
Enforced formal speech. – It's a shame, said the manager
On hearing the news. And, yes, we miss your disdain.

ALLEGRIA

What is this impulse
It's an annihilating movement
But it's also
Joy stripped of content.

What is this impulse that sends you hurtling down
The stairs, missing out the steps of regular breath
When breathing in 'hee,' breathing out 'haw' until you reach the springboard
Street? – Note that I'm not asking
Where that step comes from, too light
For anything to be placed on it, not even a question.
I'd like to name it in memory of a rather offbeat
Dialogue in which words got carried off with
The sheets of the block where they'd been neatly aligned
Knocked over by a gust of wind. – Out
Of our sight! words incapable
Of containing the pathos-less emotion of the wind:
The wind because what exactly were we talking about
Wielding neologisms and heavier periphrases
To capture finer nuances? – Of nothing at all
That's the point. Oh well it's the same today
If I ask you what you're thinking of, you cling on
Intent to run the length of an endless spiral
To whatever rail, thick presence, central pillar, anything
That prevents life going off course: certainty here
And now or subject of conversation. – Nothing!
Anyhow it was enough to ask the question
As you drop a sheet before the blades at the end

Of a line to see if it'll take off at the beginning
Of the next. – At the moment you rebound
From the pavement following the last step
You're no more than a photogram and the landscape with you
Frozen by the pause button on the videotape player
But one that doesn't want to stop, trembles like a leaf
Or a trapped rodent struggling to rejoin
Its fellows. The image too wants to enter into the dance
Of images/second. What is this impulse that
Outmodes all deposits, parked cars
Buildings unharmed by the night's bombardments
And waking resolutions? From any point of view,
Whether exterior hidden in the landscape
Crossed abolished as a sniper keeps his gun trained on you
To avenge the universe to which you're directing this dirty trick
Or inside, your vision stripped of its reference points,
It's an annihilating movement, climb and abject fall
An inextinguishable thirst, a repeated call
For sacrifice (and I add to this on purpose), it accelerates
Devastation. – But it's also
Just the opposite this one-way trip
That nothing can justify. Not a pleasure
For it gets you nothing and each moment deprives you
Of the spectacle wrapped into the rear-view mirror
Gaze fixed on the stub of road lunging
At you. Joy stripped of content:
The visible idea of dance in the mirror
That has consumed the wall behind the projectors emptying

The floor of its dancers in training too concerned
About where their right foot is (upbeat) and their left
At the back and to the side (downbeat) to admire their own
Twirls. Gone for good like you
Parisians of a long-exposed photo by Atget
Speeding did they at least experience orgasm
In a sneeze? – The stroboscope resuscitates them
As dancers, fugitives, ghosts caught on the run
Time enough to recognize them as brothers in arms
Then we'll have to pick up other combustible images
Burn the furniture until we find the explosive
Dose of absence, joy and movement.

PARALLEL LIVES

Panes of glass slide one over the other
Slices of life
The exponential tree
Of a novel-in-which-you're-not-the-hero
Paths that are corridors
Not to choose between
Borrowed identities
Like dromomaniacs
Passing from one line to another
Every action triggers a parallel life.

It's a necklace of coloured pearls
The more you add, of course, the less easily you make out
The thread but the child can't get over it
Hanging from the lady's neck
The sky forms two panels
That lean towards the summit of the portico
And curved Earth a launch-
Pad. He laughs
As though demented at the game
Of continuity and discontinuity
Two points of view on the light
Two reading speeds. Outside
The town takes up this motif
Ad nauseam flattening it out
Panes of glass slide one over the other
Transparent slices of life
Perfectly enigmatic.
You can follow a passer-by, the beginning of a story

Jump from a moving train, take
Another but surfing like that will daze you
Without piercing the mystery or indeed
You could take up position in one of those strategic places
In fiction where things happen –
Cable let's say – and watch
The little windows
Of competing channels blink.

Fiction feeds on lateness:
At first you're on time, then just there
Then you wait, then play the waiting game
That loads the future like an accomplice
On the run and stocks their file with crimes
Ultimately unrealistic, each minute
Vies in cruelty to paint disasters
Incompatible of course, say knocked over
By a bus she'll turn up on the arm
Of her new lover: the exponential tree
With false clues and blatant repercussions
Of a novel-in-which-you're-not-the-hero so that
The latecomers fearing to confront a mindless fault-finding
Gaze are mistaken, we rediscover them
Escaped, acquitted though only just, we read
As we would an actor's face
The network of features of every script
Of the B-movies they've starred in without knowing it
For half an hour and we say: Ah it's you.

Or in interminable discussions at night
Following paths that are corridors
Between two walls of blackened leaves
Words in the forest of hypotheses
Whose detours bring to light
Buried regrets, insanely ramified torments
And skeletons unearthed for the good of the cause
To the interlocutor either more and more downcast or
Furious as the bids rise
Before the negotiations have begun – will it be
War or peace after all? For the moment
Perspective, delimited by myopia
Dug into by the little light, sows
Glimmers like bits of mirror
And neither side must carry it off
Because it's not a tragedy in which everyone's right
But ordinary atrocity in which no one's wrong
For the wrong reasons. The intertwined rails
At the end of that tunnel have been engraved in memory
Since dawn when the switchman opened the gates
Fast track or siding, engraved like the stamp
Of the genie that presided with complicated and violent thoughts
Over the meeting of those two
For a discussion in bed at night.

It's enough not to choose.
What could be more beautiful than a diving suit?
And what can be said after that? If perfection was

Achieved elsewhere or glimpsed rising from the bath
Useless to imitate it, fool around
Rather rags and better not to choose between
Borrowed identities same difference twice over
Let them insist on their little differences in cut,
Play the generous soul, version *no look*.
The clothes are ultra-important, which is to say the camouflaged
Combat gear composed of bits of uniforms
Feathers of mechanical birds and false tree-leaves
Taken from parallel regiments, ah to desert
Betray without betraying oneself like dromomaniacs
Passing from one line to another with such natural ease.
It's enough not to act.

What could be more beautiful than these empty slots in the middle
Of a film or sequence of events
Set off by the word action
The décor dilates
And the light
Freed
Click
Becomes more tangible as the accessories
Invade the screen the vanishing lines
Slide to each corner the characters
Unoccupied watch each other
And their words
Echo-less
Smack

The story was suspended but continues elsewhere
With the same actors the same voices
Watch it they're ghosts
Continuing to roam
For they didn't hear
Anyone say
Cut
The originals stay there free immobile
And see themselves in action as in a dream
Edited brutally
A parallel life
Made of high
Points and of
Falls
For every action unfolds outside of you
Every action triggers a parallel life
But for the spectators the wait
Replaces each object
In its aura
Shows it in its true
Light.

Finally we woke up schizophrenic.

The metal shutter falls on the inside
When sleep half-advanced lets go of
Your hand in front of a café window
And a few chairs champ at the bit in the corners

Of the walled room that is a dream
Interrupted scattered with empty packets
In the right-hand side of the brain separated from the left
Where the town detaches itself with difficulty
Two aborted worlds side by side
One inside already closed the other outside where
It's not yet opening time.

HYPERAUBADE

Nothing has happened but the transition
From night to day to night that's all.

It will be like that from now on
The moon has grown I say the moon but
I could just as well say something else
Totalizing and banal a muscle man
Instead of exploding it has faded
Beneath our red nocturnal animal eyes

Flat disorder definitively
Gains the upper hand when you lack good tools the blade
That hones sense and then the needle
That sews paradox

              You wanted
Sharpened contours clean shadows
To track a perfumed lonce
In which night takes shape a muscular
Mass and leaps beyond itself

It was a form of dream that simultaneously
Installs chaos and
Intensifies it before morning

Instead came the aqueous day
Lacking solution the remnants float above it

In a calm lapping a regular arrhythmia
In which e's proliferate
Silently alongside computer viruses

What to hope for if the mood falls like that
Disappearing behind the prostheses
And the sounds emitted by the worm-eaten structure
It's lying low the mood hiding
From fear of a new collapse

During the day the mechanical tumult
Soothes and the town generates smoke
That muffles it at the height of expenditure
A diversion that no longer deceives anyone

Nothing has happened but the transition
From night to day to night that's all
The night polishing the days
Mechanics just that little bit more

                Let's slow down
You were speaking of chaos and sadness
Of form that saves and good tools
But again

                We're afraid no longer know
What we're saying 'we' becomes the dubious form
Of that inhuman eye that sweeps the shadow

III

Where the luminous swarm disperses
Prey with last evening's heat

However good the surveyor's tools may be
The located point dissolves in the flux
Form escapes and nothing with it
Attacked on all sides it flees suddenly re-assembled
A feline with a brilliant black gaze
Fiancée of chaos

Is it sad
This fall back into the junk room
Mood belongs to fixed beauty or the storm
According to how much it expects from the day
The glimmer it so obstinately refuses

For it overexposes the landscape
And hides away all those who pass through it
Stowaways of images revealed
In the bath of infrared light
More real than nature more violent
But unfixed

It will be like that
Every morning we'll have to return
To throw empty bottles into the hole
And sing with voices of unpolished glass
A morning song to entropy.

Born in Paris in 1963, French poet, novelist, and translator, Pierre Alferi is the author of some twelve books of poetry as well as five novels and four works in film. A frequent collaborator with musicians, visual artists, and film makers, he has worked extensively to develop the genre of the cinépoème and the short lyric film. He's also the translator of an unusually wide range of writers, from John Donne to George Oppen, and the co-founder of two literary journals, *Détail*, with Suzanne Doppelt, and *La Revue de Littérature Générale*, with Olivier Cadiot. He teaches in Paris at the École des Arts Décoratifs and at the École des Beaux-Arts, and in Saas-Fee, Switzerland at the European Graduate School.

Kate Lermitte Campbell recently completed a DPhil at Oxford University. The title of her dissertation was *Thought, Perception and the Creative Act: A Study of the Work of Four Contemporary French Poets: Pierre Alferi, Valère Novarina, Anne Portugal and Christophe Tarkos*. She lives and works in London and Paris.

Night and Day is the tenth title in the La Presse series of contemporary French poetry in translation. The series is edited by Cole Swensen and designed by Shari DeGraw. This book is typeset in Adobe Jenson.